Praise for Oscar Fuentes' *Honey & Sting*

"In *Honey & Sting*, Oscar Fuentes' confessional poems and stories sing in perfect rhythm to his aching heart. A touch Neruda, a touch Holman, and a touch Monet, Fuentes flexes his poetic muscles to deliver a genre-bending oeuvre sure to resonate with poets, musicians, and the masses. Buy this beautiful book. You won't regret it!"
— Nicole Tallman, Author of *Poems for the People*

"Dancing expertly between hilarity and absurdity, tenderness, regret, raunchiness and family love, the range of emotions and experiences depicted in *Honey & Sting* reveal the heart and mind of a vivid consciousness enthusiastically alive to the vicissitudes of life in 2023 Miami. Once again, Oscar Fuentes, "The Biscayne Poet," pricks his readers awake with his penetrating insights and attention to the aching range of our various desires--and the ways these desires affect behavior and culture, dreams and memory. These wildly entertaining and moving works celebrate our common humanity in all its glory, funkiness, hunger, and grief. Though written in prose, these writings sing like true poetry."
— Michael Hettich, Author of *The Halo of Bees: New and Selected Poems, 1990-2022*

"'Will you receive my tongue like a pregnant pope?' asks Oscar Fuentes in his new collection. 'Yes,' you answer. And unlock the Secrets of the Universe."
— Bob Holman, Founder of Bard of the Bowery Poetry

"With *Honey & Sting*, Oscar Fuentes, otherwise known as the Biscayne Poet, plays with the universal themes of trauma and chaos by subtly planting them in uniquely exotic narratives involving cock fights and zebras from Korea. The playfulness of his approach reminds the reader that in darkness you can find the creativity of transcendence and that your strength comes from your roots."
— Renzo Del Castillo, Author of *Still*

"Only poetic hearts risk getting stung in pursuit of love's sweet rewards. So who'd dare judge if, on occasion, a stiff drink or three are imbibed to help muster the requisite courage to enter this perennial battlefield and live to write about it in valiantly vulnerable verse? For, to know the heights of love—be it romantic, familial, or otherwise—is, invariably and inevitably, to know pain and loss. Some are called to create art out of our traumas and tragedies. Rare, however, are the artists who also manage to make us laugh at their own expense. Fortunately, for those who prefer to live vicariously, or those in need of an everyman hero whose fears and foibles are not unlike our own, we've got Oscar Fuentes, aka "The Biscayne Poet." With his fingers firmly on the pulse of Miami's tropical, urban milieu, Oscar pours his passion into each story and poem with an abandoned commensurate with his incorrigible but lovable heart and the place he calls home. And as we, his readers, follow his mischievous antics, the city's sensuality, and idiosyncrasies seep into our imaginations. Along the way, we just might find ourselves buoyed by the beat of his verse and the example of a life lived to the fullest."
— Joshua Mapp Weiss, Founder of HeartPlay

"*Honey & Sting* is a playful, confessional, and heartwarming collection of poetry that gives readers a little bit of everything. Camouflaging depth with description and detail, Oscar Fuentes showcases the beauty, pain, and truth, of being an artist, a poet, and a human being."
— Flor Ana, Author of *A Moth Fell In Love With The Moon*

HONEY & STING
POEMS AND SHORT STORIES

OSCAR FUENTES
THE BISCAYNE POET

Cover Photography Copyright © 2023 by Marcello Cassano
Cover Design Copyright © 2023 by Micah Marie Johnson
Edited by Flor Ana Mireles, Carmen Mise Fuentes, and Oscar Musibay

1st Edition | 01
Paperback ISBN: 979-8-9880379-2-7

First Published August 2023

For inquiries and bulk orders, please email:
indieearthbooks@gmail.com

Printed in the United States of America   1 2 3 4 5 6 7 8 9

Indie Earth Publishing Inc.
| Miami, FL |

www.indieearthbooks.com

Honey & Sting

Poems and Short Stories

Oscar Fuentes
AKA
The Biscayne Poet

Acknowledgments

Within the pages of *Honey & Sting*, I embarked on a journey to conceal my personal trauma. I scattered fragments of my pain, shattered into countless pieces, throughout the stories and poems in this humble collection. It was an attempt to mask the depth of my experiences, believing that, by diluting them, I could find relief and healing.

I recognize that even though I may feel somewhat prepared to delve into the realm of personal issues and childhood traumas, I am merely scratching the surface. The courage I mustered to weave into my characters' experiences is just the beginning, a springboard for further exploration and understanding.

In the stories that revolve around my family, I tried to summon my inner strength to confront the layers of passing years, like a mound of forgotten memories concealing the most painful ones beneath. It was an act of persuasion, an urging for my resilience to face the shadows that haunt me.

I want to express my gratitude to those who have accompanied me on this confessional journey. Your presence and support mean more to me than I can put into words. As readers, your engagement with my creative writing fuels my determination to continue unraveling the complexities of my personal narrative.

Moreover, I want to extend my appreciation to the individuals who have shared fragments of their own stories, inspiring me to delve deeper and confront my own truths. It is through these collective experiences that we find solace, understanding, and the courage to heal.

I want to send a big thank you to my advanced readers who are also my friends—poets and writers I admire and who have also influenced my work in so many ways: Nicole Tallman, Aja Monet, Bob Holman, Michael Hettich, Josh Weiss, Oscar Musibay, Paul Lunaire, Renzo Del Castillo, and Flor Ana.

I want to thank my publisher, Indie Earth Publishing, and my editor, Flor Ana Mireles, for guiding me through the muddy process of finalizing this project. I also want to thank Marcello Cassano as well as Micah Marie Johnson for the photography and cover design of this collection.

I also want to send a bigger than life thank you to my beautiful family: Mom, Dad, Carlo, Gissel, Katia, Andres, Marcos, Sophy, Emily, Victoria, and Camila.

Lastly, I thank my wife, Carmen Mise Fuentes, who has always supported and encouraged my creative spirit. Without her patience, love, and advice, *Honey & Sting* wouldn't exist.

Honey & Sting is an invitation to explore the depths of human emotion and resilience. As you immerse yourself in these stories and poems, I hope they serve as catalysts for introspection, encouraging you to confront your own buried pain and uncover the strength that lies within.

Honey & Sting

Poems and Short Stories

Oscar Fuentes

For my grandmother

Foreword
By Oscar Musibay

Oscar Fuentes just wrote "Love is Evil," and I'm in love with the full-throttle passion that comes from a life lived. The street stories are a concussion-fueled, meteoric, color-drenched explosion that makes the Big Bang look like a tale told by romantic, heartbroken astronomers. Love ripped out from your chest and stomped on.

"...In the end, love is a lie disguised as a painful truth after all the sweet sex has ended." Can it be any more raw? Not unless the butcher lives in your building and is waiting to make sloppy work of the "Lizard Landlord," who roams the halls demanding rent, his gun visible for all to see.

"La Cantina Negra" is a story of desire and dislocation and how obsession can warp the heart and scar the mind. The main character's pain is now, visceral, like licking a razor blade before swallowing the salt and biting the lime.

So, why wouldn't the hero hide from the world in the Cadillac bed when it makes him feel like settling down and staying forever? Because the Boulevard calls, stirring something wild and restless inside, and we get to enjoy the ride.

If you ask Oscar Fuentes, who goes by The Biscayne Poet, he might tell you his cock fighting stories about circuses and the humble man making the ring out of chairs. He covered the floor with cedar chips and sawdust. What was the wife of the ringleader doing? Read "The Cock Fight" to find out.

The brutal struggle to learn and heal joins with hope in several of his stories, encouraging the reader to open the next door. In "Sand Between My Teeth," Oscar's voice is born again on the beach during a party, the revelers welcoming him with open arms.

Can it be that simple, that community and love are the secret to happiness? The opportunity to answer the question is offered in "The Brooklyn Bridge Story," which brings the reader along as the hero and his friends celebrate "our victory over the bridge." Read carefully to learn the truth.

"Truth is, no one knows the way you do. Ain't that something?" he whispered, looking into her eyes. But what was her response, dear writer?

For Oscar Fuentes, writing is about hope, longing and community. Life is the story; you can choose the lines you add to it. If you haven't noticed, these stories kill fascists, paraphrasing Woody Guthrie. Rise up from your knees, pick up a pen, typewriter, or computer, and give it your best shot!

Oscar Musibay, aka Varadero the Writer, is an award-winning journalist and a lover of the written and spoken word.
He feels fortunate to call Oscar Fuentes a friend and brother.

Contents

Contents

Honey & Sting

Poems and Short Stories

Oscar Fuentes

As you immerse yourself in *Honey & Sting*, I hope you will find comfort and resonance within the creative turbulence of these pages. May these stories and poems serve as a reminder that our emotions, even in their darkest and most chaotic forms, hold the potential for catharsis and growth.

Growing Up

The Biscayne Poet

Guayaba Tree

That guava tree at Abuela Fina's house was my playground, my refuge, my everything. I literally grew up on those branches, spending endless afternoons jumping off them, picking ripe guavas, and waiting for Abuelo Carlos to arrive from work.

Those afternoons were golden, so vivid in my mind, even now. I remember the thrill of screaming out Abuelo's name when his bus arrived, and the joy of seeing him wave back at me. I remember the taste of those hand-picked guavas, sweet and juicy, bursting with flavor. And I remember the smell of Abuela Fina's cooking, wafting from the kitchen, calling us home for dinner.

Those dinners were always a feast, with Abuela's delicious homemade flour tortillas, refried beans, and all the other treats she would whip up. The flavors were so familiar, so comforting, so uniquely hers. I can still taste them if I close my eyes. But it was that guava tree that defined those afternoons, that made them magical. It was a place of endless possibilities, where I could be whoever I wanted to be, where I could escape the world and just be a kid. I remember climbing to the top, feeling the breeze on my face, and looking out over the world, feeling like anything was possible.

And when Abuela Fina called us for dinner, I would jump off that tree, landing with a thud on the soft earth below, and run inside, my stomach growling with hunger. It was a simpler time, a time of innocence and wonder. A time when that guava tree was the center of my world.

Now, as an adult, I realize how much that tree meant to me, how it shaped me, how it gave me a sense of belonging and home. And even though it's gone now, chopped down by someone who didn't understand its value, its memory lives on in me. That guava tree will always be a part of who I am, a reminder of the golden afternoons of my childhood, and the love and warmth of Abuela Fina's home.

Abuela Fina

It's been years since Abuela Fina left us, but her memories still flood my mind every day. She was more than just a grandmother to me; she was a friend, a protector, and a guiding light that illuminated my path.

Growing up with Abuela Fina was like living in a different world. It was a world where time moved slower, where the rain was never a nuisance but a blessing, and where the sun was always warm and welcoming. It was a world where crime and fear were just words we heard on TV but never experienced.

Abuela Fina made that world possible. She loved me unconditionally and made me feel like I was the most important person in the world. She would take me to the park, teach me how to cook, and tell me stories about my ancestors. She always carried an umbrella with her, not just to protect us from the rain, but as a symbol of her unwavering love and protection.

When she passed away, I didn't cry, and I still don't know why. Maybe it was because I was too young to understand the finality of death. Or maybe it was because I believed she would always be there, sheltering me from the rain and the troubles of the world.

Now, as an adult, I realize how lucky I was to have her in my life. She taught me how to be kind, how to be strong, and how to love unconditionally. She gave me a sense of belonging and showed me that family is not just blood but the people who love you and care for you.

Abuela Fina may be gone, but her legacy lives on in me and in the memories I hold dear. I will always be grateful for the time I spent with her, and I will always cherish the world she created for me.

A Forgotten Friend

Oscar Sr. took a ride on his bike. Gloria had decided to take the bus because she felt too old to ride on the bike with Oscar.

The humble light blue house of Josefina, Gloria's mother, was six miles away from their house. They both had gone to visit the old folks, for it had been a while since they last saw each other. Josefina had been sick for quite a long while, and she had gotten the flu, bad. Her knees had gone weak and the veins on her legs had gotten thick and blue, sometimes purple, but her daughter had gone over with Oscar, and she was going to be okay.

Gloria had gone to nursing school and she really knew how to handle the injection needle. Who knows exactly how many injections she had given to people; everyone in their neighborhood knew she was a certified nurse, and most of them had gone to her house once or twice for an injection or two.

But now, Gloria found herself inside her mother's house, the same exact house that she had lived in ever since she was a little girl. Now, after fifty-some years, Gloria found herself in the old house, and as she injected the antibiotic into her mother's left arm, Gloria thought about her childhood. She thought about the many little details engraved in her memory. The walls of her mother's house, the old tile floor, the old high ceiling, her long lost friends, her five sisters and her two brothers. She thought about them as little girls and boys and she thought about time, how it had gone by so fast. Gloria thought about her three kids and how each of the three had started their familes. She thought about Oscar Jr. and his pregnant girlfriend, and the baby boy inside her belly.

"What are you thinking about, Mama?" Josefina would ask.

"My son. I'm thinking about my son."

"Which one? Carlos?"

"No. Oscar. Wow, I can't believe he's having a baby boy."

"Yeah, me neither."

Gloria had already injected the antibiotic into her mother's arm and an hour had passed since she had arrived at the old house.

"Look, there comes your husband."

"Where?"

"There," Josefina pointed with her right arm toward the outside; her left arm felt numb, with a constant electrical shock of pain.

Gloria looked through the windows and kept her eyes on Oscar.

Oscar rode his bike down the little hill where the main street pavement had been laid out, about fifty feet in front of Josefina's old house.

He rode on, maneuvering his bicycle, and stopped it right at the front gate of the house. He got off it, parked it under the tropical shade of an almond tree, opened the front gate slowly, and walked in under the tin roof of the front porch of the house.

Oscar walked into the house through the front door feeling out of breath. His legs felt weak and sweat slowly ran down both sides of his forehead.

"You had worried there for a moment, my love," Gloria said to him.

"Oh, I'm okay, my princess. It had been a while since I last rode that bicycle."

"I know," Gloria replied.

"Why don't you sit down and rest? I'll make you some good coffee," Josefina said.

"Thank you," Oscar replied.

He sat down on Josefina's old comfortable couch and took a deep breath; he then gave a sigh.

Josefina, with caution, took a step down onto the kitchen floor, which was at a lower level than the living room floor, and started heating the water for coffee. Gloria and Oscar sat by themselves under the living room ceiling and looked at each other. Gloria smiled at him. He smiled at her. They both had puppy eyes and it was obvious that their love was now stronger than ever.

After a while, Josefina walked into the living room and handed Oscar his warm cup of good Honduran coffee. She sat down next to him on the couch. Gloria sat on one of the chairs of the dining table, and the three of them talked and laughed for a good while. After five whole hours, the three of them felt tired, and Oscar and Gloria decided that it was time for them to leave and head on over to their small house.

They both kissed and hugged Josefina. Gloria gave her an extra hug and they embraced tightly for a moment. Meanwhile, Oscar stood outside the house, under the tropical cool shade of Josefina's almond tree and thought about his cockfighting chickens. He thought about training them some more, and he also thought about taking them to competitions. All his life, Oscar had been a fanatic of the cock fight. He owned seventy-two fighting roosters, and sixty-three fighting hens.

Finally, Gloria came out of her mother's house, and out through the front gate she went, closing it behind her.

"Are you taking the bus again?" Oscar asked her.

"Do you want me to go with you?" she asked.

"Only if you want, but it's a long ride. Maybe you should take the bus."

"Okay, I'll take the bus."

"I'll walk you to the bus stop."

They both started walking towards the main street hill, and halfway there, they both turned around and looked at the house, as if looking for Josefina, and she was there, standing behind the front gate of her house, under the tin roof of her porch. Gloria and Oscar waved at her. Josefina waved back. They kept on walking and started climbing the hill. They reached the main street and crossed it, making sure there were no cars coming on either side. They got to the bus stop. Oscar parked the bicycle over on the side. He held Gloria's hand. Gloria held his. They both kissed, smiled, and waited for the bus to come.

After a moment of waiting, the bus finally came. Gloria got in and paid her fare. The bus started moving forward. She looked out through the windows and looked for her husband. He was still there, standing and waiting for her to look at him. He knew she would, and she had. They both stared at each other and smiled. Oscar waved, but Gloria did not, and her bus was now very far away, heading towards their neighborhood.

Oscar unlocked the parking pedal of the bicycle, and walked and pushed the bike a little. Then, he hopped on it and started pedaling. He was in motion, slowly gaining speed. Now, he was going fast, fast enough to feel and hear the wind in his ears.

Between Josefina's house and the house Gloria and Oscar owned, there were six miles of sugarcane plantation. While riding his bicycle, Oscar settled at a comfortable pedaling rhythm and worked on it without even noticing. There was a nice fresh afternoon feel to the air and Oscar had not even started to sweat. He had rested his knees for five whole hours and they didn't feel weak. Instead, they felt strong. His knees felt young and light.

He rode his bike on the narrow side of the main street that was dusty and kept the road to himself, making sure not to ride on the main road because this part of town had a reputation of bad drivers.

Oscar Sr. had always preferred his bike ride over the bus ride because he knew too many people—or should I say, too many people knew him—and to avoid the small talk, he'd take the long way because the long way was lonely, quiet, and peaceful. He also used that peace and all that pedaling to deal with his own demons, the childhood trauma inflicted by his father, who had been an orphan and had been physically abused and traumatized by the different families that raised him with an iron fist. But the pedaling helped a lot, and the wind was truly peaceful and calming, and he had healed his childhood scars a whole lot through the years.

Halfway from his house, in the middle of that entire sugarcane plantation, Oscar stopped pedaling, and slowly, his bicycle stopped moving. It had been a long day, full of nothing. No action. The sun looked good, giant, and orange. He felt a little bit out of breath, but that was okay.

Right where Oscar had stopped, right there in the middle of the road and sugarcanes, Oscar gave deep sighs and thought about his kids. Gloria's kids were the same kids that Oscar would think of whenever he thought of his kids, and now Oscar thought of the youngest one, Carlos, who had recently moved out of the house and into this small simple place he and his girlfriend had found on the skirt of Merendon Mountain.

The orange Central American sun was going down slow and majestic, and Oscar loved to catch the sun on the way down. Every day around this same time, Oscar made sure to be out in the open, looking up toward the sun, but he would never look straight at the sun. Instead, he enjoyed the mixture of colors in the Central American sky around this time in the afternoon.

Today the sky looks nicer than yesterday, Oscar thought, and while thinking that, he noticed how it was getting dark and late.

So, he pushed his bicycle and hopped on it, and kept on traveling towards his house. The colors in the sky were fading, and the sky was now not-so pretty, and Oscar knew this. But still, he kept on looking up while riding the old horse.

Then, Oscar heard a voice. The voice came from behind him. Oscar turned his head and looked back. There behind him came someone riding on a bicycle, but the person was too far and Oscar could not get a clear look at the face.

"Oscar!" the person called again.

Oscar looked again and decided to come to a complete stop. He turned around and waited for the person that called his name twice. It was an old man that looked familiar to him, but he couldn't make out who.

Then, the man spoke to him again and Oscar recognized him with a smile.

The Cantina Negra

A short story

Chapter One: *Sofia. Music. Love. Desire.*

The musicians came out and began tuning loudly. I glanced at my watch, seeing it was already ten o'clock. The small man in the pink suit stood behind the microphone at the center of the stage, adjusted it for his height, and spoke just as the waiter returned with our drinks.

"Good evening, ladies, and gentlemen! Welcome to La Cantina Negra. Tonight, we have an excellent show for everyone. Please feel free to get up and dance to the hypnotizing rhythm of our beautiful Sofia!"

The musicians began a mambo. Sofia, emerging from stage left wearing a beautiful feathery dress, walked up to the announcer, kissed his cheek, and waited while he adjusted the mic stand for her before walking off.

She raised her arms up in a V, and all the musicians stopped. Taking the cordless mic, she removed it from the stand and began singing softly without accompaniment.

I guessed her age at twenty-five. She had long, thick, firm legs, and her voice was like Ella Fitzgerald's. I couldn't take my eyes off her. All I wanted was a hot bath with her beside me near a giant window overlooking the ocean, a bottle of Dom Perignon, Esther Phillips playing softly in the background, and a thick sponge to scrub those sexy legs slowly.

I had fallen in love, and no one knew it. I sat there, mesmerized by Sofia's voice as she sang her heart out on the stage. The mambo beat had picked up, and the entire crowd was dancing and swaying to the rhythm. Sofia's voice was the star of the show, soaring above the music and filling the entire room with a sense of passion and longing. As the night went on, Sofia sang hit after hit, each one more beautiful than the last. Her stage presence was undeniable, and her energy seemed to flow out of her and into the audience. People were laughing, dancing, and enjoying themselves like they never had before.

But for me, the night was about more than just the music. It was about Sofia herself. She was captivating, with a smile that lit up the room and a voice that could make you forget your troubles. I couldn't help but wonder what it would be like to spend time with her, to get to know her intimately. As the night wore on, I found myself growing more and more enamored with Sofia. I wanted to talk to her, to tell her how I felt. But I was too nervous, too afraid of what she might say. So, I just sat there, watching her from a distance, hoping that maybe, just maybe, she might feel the same way.

Eventually, the night came to an end, and Sofia took her final bow. The crowd roared with applause as she walked offstage, and I knew that I would never forget this night, or Sofia's incredible performance. As I walked out of La Cantina Negra, the memory of Sofia's voice still ringing in my ears and in my heart, I had already decided. I was going to find a way to see her again, to talk to her, to tell her how I felt. And who knows? Maybe one day we could be together, bathed in the soft light of the moon, listening to Esther Phillips, and enjoying each other's company.

Chapter Two: *Rewind to Maria.*

I walked into our hotel room, and I could hear Maria in the shower. The room was not bad. A medium sized kitchen. A small dining room. A small living room with a sofa, flat screen TV, coffee table, and a wooden chair. Not bad at all. Two large windows showed you the infinity of the ocean. A beautiful breath-taking view. You could see the windsurfers playing with the waves. A cargo ship sliding away over there at the end of it all.

There was a wooden dresser with a wide tall mirror. A small table next to the bed with a bottle of Mezcal on top of it. Next to the bottle was this small plastic cup with sliced limes, a saltshaker, and two shot glasses. I served myself a shot. Put some salt on the palm of my hand. Squeezed a piece of lime into the shot glass. I heard Maria turn off the shower. I licked the salt off the palm of my hand and took the shot right after.

Maria came out of the bathroom with her pink towel-like robe on. She looked very sexy. Her robe was short. Very short. Almost like a mini skirt robe. I gave her the *I want you* look. She gave me the *come and get it* look. I started to undress and while I did that, Maria walked over to the small table and served herself a shot, drank it down without salt or lime.

I was now naked and under the sheets. You could see my friendly ghost sticking up, making a tent out of the flowery blanket. Maria unleashed the robe and climbed in next to me. We fell asleep after sex and when we woke up, it was already dark outside. We looked out from the window, and it was still there, the immense ocean and the moon sneaking up slowly.

Maria looked at me and started to laugh. She was laughing hysterically. God, she laughed so much that she even released gas. That's when I started to laugh. When she released little bits of gas that made noise. We would look at each other and laugh. We would look out the window and laugh. Laugh. Laugh. Laugh. God, we felt so happy laughing.

For the past three months, Maria and I had been having horrible arguments. Most of them were my fault. We would both annoy the shit out of each other, and one of us would always end up leaving the house for a few hours. The arguments always got loud and nasty; in the middle of them, I would always end up breaking something. A mirror. A plate. A coffee mug. A broom stick, or just about anything breakable that was right there at the reach of my hand. But now, we were OK. Laughing naked in bed. No arguments. No screaming. No hatred. Only love. Love and pleasure.

In fifteen minutes, I was dressed and perfumed. Maria wasn't dressed, and her hair was not done. I figured it would take her an hour to get ready, so I decided to go downstairs to the lobby and ask about local bars with live music. Before I left the room, I reached over to the little table and took hold of the Mezcal bottle and a shot glass. I poured the Mezcal into the shot glass; I noticed a dead yellow worm floating at the bottom of the bottle. I took the shot, and I told Maria I was going to be back in a few.

I was now in the lobby and the man behind the check-in desk was the same man that had checked us in earlier. There was now a woman next to him. She had dirty blonde hair and a tight green dress that was very long. It went all the way down to her ankles. I approached them.

"Mr. Fuentes, how may I help you?"

"Know of a good place to eat, have a few drinks, live music?"

"Oh, La Cantina Negra, around the corner, it's a very nice place," the woman responded.

"Yes, Mr. Fuentes, that's the place where the beautiful Sofia performs," said the man pointing at her and looking at her with puppy eyes.

"Really?" I said, feeling a bit curious.

"Yes, Mr. Fuentes, if you go tonight, I will dedicate the show to you and your wife."

"Oh, that would be very kind of you, I'm sure we'll enjoy it," I said to her.

She looked deep into my eyes as if looking for something. I could tell she didn't want the guy to find out she was looking at me the way she was. I gave no reaction to her staring.

"Well then, thank you, Sofia. At what time does the show begin?"

"At ten, the show begins at 10:00 pm," the man responded.

"Sounds good, see you both at ten."

I left them alone. I went back to the room and Maria was beginning to blow-dry her hair. I sat on the edge of the bed next to the dead worm, took off my shoes and looked out the windows. The full moon. The large windows. Maria was blow-drying her hair. The towel that covered her breasts. Her hair hung all the way down to her thick tanned thighs. Half her ass uncovered. Her dark, long sexy legs. Her staring at me through the mirror. I felt happiness.

Maria was almost done drying her long black strips of hair. I looked at the worm inside the bottle. I stared at it for a moment. With my thoughts, I tried to communicate with the dead insect, but there was no reply. Then, I turned my head and looked at Maria's legs. I looked at her curves. Then, I looked at her legs again. And then, my eyes focused on her beautiful round ass. I stared at it for a moment. I started getting excited. I kept on looking at it.

Then, I screamed, "I'LL EAT YOU TOO!! JUST LIKE THE WORM!"

Maria jumped.

"What the hell was that?" she asked, laughing.

"Oh no, don't mind me, I'm just talking to myself here while I wait," I said to her, smiling.

I turned to look at the bottle. Grabbed it. Poured some Mezcal onto the shot glass. Brought the shot glass to my lips and drank it down. Served myself another and poured one for Maria. I drank mine in one gulp, Maria drank hers in two.

Maria was finally dressed and perfumed. She looked good. She had gotten dressed to impress. She was wearing a tight glittering short black dress with black, six-inch heels. I served myself two more shots, and the goddamn worm was still there at the bottom of the bottle.

I grabbed the key to the room and walked out. She followed me. I locked the room and we started toward the lobby. We didn't say a word to each other on our way to Cantina Negra. We just walked in silence, holding hands.

At Cantina Negra, we were sitting on these comfortable brown leather chairs with wooden arms. Our table was round with a white tablecloth over it. We sat three tables away from the stage and one table away from the middle aisle. There was a long bar next to the entrance of the place. On stage, you could see a drum set, three microphone stands, a trumpet inside an opened trumpet casing, a pair of conga drums, and maracas. A small man in a pink suit was working on the sound check.

The waiter came to our table and Maria ordered two margaritas, and the waiter went to get them. The musicians started tuning their instruments loud. I looked at my watch and it was already 10:00 pm. The small man in the pink suit stood behind the main microphone stand in the center of the stage. He adjusted the stand so that the mic would be right there in front of his lips, then he spoke as the waiter came back with our drinks.

"Good evening, ladies, and gentlemen, and welcome to La Cantina Negra. Tonight, we have an excellent show for everyone. Please feel at home and feel free to get up from your seats and dance to the rhythm of our BEAUTIFUL SOFIA!!"

The musicians started beating and blowing on their instruments. The music was loud. It sounded like mambo music. Then, from the stage-left, Sofia came out wearing a feathery dress. BEAUTIFUL. Just plain beautiful. She walked up to the small man in pink. Gave him a kiss on the cheek. He adjusted the mic-stand for her and walked off.

She raised her arms up in the air making a V. The musicians simultaneously stopped playing. Sofia took hold of the cordless mic and snapped it out of its stand. She began to sing softly without the musicians. Her legs were long, thick, and firm. Her voice was very much like the voice of Ella Fitzgerald. Enchanting. Sexy. God, I couldn't take my eyes off her. All I wanted was to take a hot bath with her next to a giant window overlooking the ocean, a bottle of Dom Perignon, Esther Phillips playing softly, and a nice thick sponge to slowly scrub those sexy legs. Love, Love. I had fallen in love, and no one knew a thing. I could feel Maria staring at me. I looked at her.

Then, she said, "Close your mouth, will ya? You look ridiculous with your mouth open."

I left my mouth open for a little more just to bother her. Then, I closed it.

Sofia, the exotic singer, sang a set of ten songs and then came the break. Maria and I had drunk three margaritas and we were now ready to eat. Maria signaled the waiter, and he came running to our table; we ordered our food. I had caught him staring at Maria a couple of times and I had also caught Maria giving him the eye, but I had decided not to say anything. Maria and I were nicely drunk, and an argument would have just spoiled it all for us.

The waiter came to our table with the food; two chicken quesadillas and two more margaritas and two Cuba-Libres. Maria got up to go to the washroom. She went into this hall where the restrooms were. Our waiter followed her into the hall. I pushed my plate of food to the side and gulped down my margarita.

"Hey there, Mr. Fuentes," Sofia said to me as she slipped into Maria's chair.

"Sofia, bravo, beautiful voice, you're truly talented," I said to her, not really knowing what else to say.

"Where is your wife?" she asked.

"Oh, the washroom."

"Do you have a pen with you, Mr. Fuentes?

"Yes, here."

She took one of my paper napkins and started writing down numbers.

"This is my room number," she pointed out on the napkin. "And this is the time I want you to come see me. Your wife should be asleep at that time."

"Yes, she should be, but Sofia, listen—"

"Don't say anything, Mr. Fuentes. I hope you can make it. See ya," she said, getting up from Maria's chair.

I watched her walk up to the stage. That's when I grabbed the napkin and took a close look at it, folded it in half, and put it away in my pant pocket. I had to meet her at 5:00 am in Room #32. I turned my head towards the hall where the washrooms were and noticed the waiter walk out of there drying his face with a napkin and fixing his shirt. He went behind the bar and served himself a drink. Then, out came Maria, and her walk was clumsy.

Sofia and her musicians began with their second set and the music was louder this time. As Maria got closer and closer, I noticed new wrinkles on her dress. It didn't fit her evenly, at least not the way it had looked before she went to the washroom. She sat down on her chair. Her hair was uncombed and the lipstick on her lips was no longer there.

"Oh, I feel so relieved, Oscar; you don't know how relaxed I feel."

"I can imagine," I told her, feeling insecure and jealous towards the waiter.

"Oh my God, I had forgotten about my food... Wow, I feel so drunk you don't even know."

I reached under the table and started feeling her long, smooth legs. Through my fingers, the memory ran, of all the times my hands had rediscovered her firm, tanned legs that had always led me to her melting gold. But now, they were a bit sweaty. I worked my hand up her outer thighs, felt on her ass and I didn't feel her panty. She was wearing it when we left the hotel, but now she wasn't, maybe the waiter was the one wearing it now.

Maria was devouring her quesadilla and her forehead was starting to sweat. Without saying a word, I got up from the table and started towards the women's restroom. The waiter was still behind the bar drying his face and neck. I could feel him looking at me as I made my way into the little hall. I swung the door open. I walked in and there were two young women fixing their hair and makeup in front of a long mirror.

"Don't mind me, ladies. I'm just looking for my wife's underwear," I told them as I knelt on the tile floor to look under the three toilets behind them.

And there it was. Just the way I had thought it would be. I got up on my feet and walked over to the last door, opened it, and there it was on the floor. I picked it up, and it was ripped. It had been ripped off her beautiful body. There was a used condom floating inside the toilet. I took a deep breath, smiled, and walked out of there. The two women were looking at me through the mirror in disbelief. I could see on their faces a look of stunned gossip and scandal, a look that they were here when it all happened.

Then, one of them turned around and asked me, "WHAT

ARE YOU GONNA DO TO HER?"

The other turned around and waited to hear what I was going to say. I looked at them for a moment.

"WELL, WHAT ARE YOU GONNA DO TO HER? ARE YOU GOING TO DIVORCE THAT BITCH OR WHAT?" said the one that had asked me before.

"Look at him, Rebecca. I think he's going to cry," said the same girl.

"Are you okay, Sir?" Rebecca asked. She looked concerned.

They both wanted to take care of me. A man who didn't know what he had until he lost it. I knew I had lost her. Maria was never a good match for me.

Out of all the women I had dated and fallen in love with, I had to marry Maria. I had always been doubtful of those that told me they loved me. I never really trusted that love they felt for me; somehow, I felt they were sleeping with other men while they were sleeping with me. For some strange alien reason, when I decided to marry Maria, I felt sure. I believed in her. I felt lucky. My friends envied me. I enjoyed showing her around because I knew she loved me. She had told me so. Her friends had told me so, but now I was here, in a women's restroom with her ripped panty in my hand. Broken in half. Disappointed. Feeling 10% human. I looked at the girls and walked out of there without saying a word.

I came out of the hall and looked to my right. The waiter was still there behind the bar. I could tell he was waiting for me to come out. He looked curious. He seemed ready to fight, but I had no beef with him. If I had been in his shoes, I would have probably done the same thing. Maria was not an ordinary woman. Perfect proportions. Beautiful face. I couldn't blame the guy. He had done what he had to. I ignored him as I walked. Maria was still there. Sofia was still there. The music was still loud. As I approached the table, I thought about my food. Thinking about it made me sick. I sat next to Maria. She had already eaten her quesadilla and half of mine as well.

"Where did you go? I missed you."

"Come on, let's get out of here."

"Where are we going?"

"Back to the hotel. I want to show you something."

"I don't wanna go to the hotel right now; let's stay a little longer," she said to me, almost begging.

"No, we need to go now, Maria. Get up from that chair."

I signaled the waiter, and he sent another waiter with the bill. I paid him cash. He took the money and left.

"You're not going to tip him?" Maria asked.

I looked her straight in the eye. Then, started toward the entrance door. Maria followed me. As we walked, I heard the music stop. I turned my head and searched for Sofia. Just about everyone now stood and whistled and put their hands together for the lovely woman on stage. I kept on walking. The waiter was there behind the bar. I caught him smiling at Maria. I turned to look at her, and she was smiling and waving goodbye. I swung the door open and now we were out in the open, only a block away from the hotel. Maria followed me. We didn't talk. The moon was still out. The stars were still there. I reached into my right front pant pocket and her ripped panties were still there. It was dark on the streets. The streetlights were out, but I was no longer in the dark. I had finally seen the light.

I still had knots in my throat. I tried to swallow, but I couldn't. I thought about the Mezcal bottle in our hotel room. I thought about the worm that sat at the bottom of that bottle. No worries. No betrayals. No nothing. I needed to be inside that bottle.

The first thing Maria did when we got to our room was vomit in the toilet. She drank too much and now all those margaritas along with the quesadillas were inside the toilet about to get flushed. Right after vomiting, she got in the shower for a moment. When she came out, I handed her a towel. I watched her dry her body. With her eyes closed, she walked up to the bed and got under the sheets.

I was sitting on the edge of the bed. I looked at my watch and it was already 1:00 am. I took off my shoes. Undressed. Got inside the shower and only turned on the hot water. I could feel the water burn the top of my head and my shoulders, but I didn't care. Life was full of unresolved commitments that end up becoming dead-end streets for most of us. The burning water was my punishment for my poor choice in women, for always pursuing the unavailable ones. I knew that Maria would never be available for me only, since the first day we met. I saw it in her, but maybe it was never her. Maybe it was me all along, meditating and asking the universe for a sweet loving woman to come my way, but in my asking, I'd leave out all the important detailed qualities in her.

I got out of the shower. I looked at my watch and it was already 3:00 am. I got under the sheets next to Maria and thought about Sofia. Maria started to snore. I closed my eyes and tried to fall asleep, but I knew I wouldn't be able to. Now I really had to go meet Sofia at 5:00 am. I got off the bed, got dressed, and sat on the living room sofa with a rum and coke in my hand, feeling ready for revenge. Our relationship automobile was already out of our control, traveling full speed on a head-on collision with a dead-end wall. I placed the ripped panty on the coffee table. At 4:45 am, I walked out of the room and looked for Room #32. I took the elevator down two floors, the doors opened, and I could instantly hear soft music playing at the end of the hallway. The music was coming from inside Room #32. She had left the door open. Esther Philips played softly. I knocked quietly.

Then, I heard Sofia's echoey voice, "Come inside, Mr. Fuentes. I'm waiting for you. Do lock the door behind you please."

Next thing I remember is waking up next to Sofia, our legs tangled under her white bed sheets. She turned to kiss my face, my forehead, my lips, my chin, and she smiled and kissed me nonstop. I was still a bit dizzy from last night's Cuba-Libres, Bacardi Rum fumes in my morning breath. I wasn't sure if I was dreaming all this with Sofia, but I quickly realized it was no dream, when her lips started kissing my feet. I had always been very ticklish on my flat feet, and she was now giving them soft little kisses, and my natural, involuntary reflexes kicked her hard on her nose.

"Aaargh!!!! What the fuck, Mr. Fuentes!!!"

"I'm so sorry, Sofia. I'm terribly ticklish on my feet. And please, call me Oscar."

She then threw herself on top of me, and we wrestled lovingly, made love for the next four hours under the white of her bed sheets.

Around 2:00 pm, Sofia and I found ourselves in her kitchen. I was fully dressed, and she had on this short Japanese robe that had me hypnotized. She had made me a delicious coffee, and, in my heart, I had already made her the love of my life. Without saying a word to each other, we sat at her kitchen table staring deep into our lustful eyes, sipping on coffee and smiling. Sofia looked even more beautiful in the morning without any make-up. I was flying back to Miami in just a few hours and her Japanese robe had already manipulated my perverted thoughts, and her hands, like two loving serpents, unbuttoned my shirt slowly and unzipped my blue jeans for her last kiss.

Back in the hotel room, I noticed Maria was already gone. There was a small handwritten note on the coffee table where I had placed the ripped panty.

The note read, "You deserve someone better. Have a good life!"

Chapter Three: *Miami memories flicker against the electric colors of the Bay, driving addicted to a dangerous love, lost on Biscayne.*

That same day, I was back in Miami. Back on Biscayne Boulevard. My Dodge Dart drove itself to Biscayne Bay just to welcome me back. The sunset colors on the Bay were electric orange and purple. With my eyes closed, I could feel the Biscayne wind reminding me I was back home. I got back in the Dart and was back on the Boulevard heading North past 36 Street. Through the rearview mirror, I could see the neon lights of the motels flickering. Stop on red. Drive on green. My memory would journey back to Sofia's lips, and then memory flashes of that bathroom scene with those girls feeling concerned for me.

Driving, I thought about the first days I had met Maria. I was stunned by her beauty and her disarming smile. I remember the time when I was addicted to her sexuality. It was a time of passion, of excitement, of danger. I met her when I was least expecting it, and from the moment I saw her, I knew she was different. She was married, but separated, and I didn't know that at the time. She gave me all the right signals, letting me know she wanted me as much as I wanted her. Stop on red. Drive on green.

Our affair was like fire, hot and intense, and we could never have enough of each other. We would always introduce ourselves to strangers as husband and wife. We were like two magnets drawn to each other, and we couldn't resist the pull. But then one day, her husband returned to her life, and she had to keep me as her secret lover. At first, it didn't bother me too much. She would escape to my place, and we would devour each other for an hour or two, and then she would leave. But little by little, it started to bother me more and more.

I wanted to spend more time with her, to be there for her, to show her how much I loved her. But she would always leave me alone and run to his arms. It was like I was addicted to her, to the feeling of being wanted, of being needed, of being desired. And I couldn't break free.

This went on for about four years, and I was slowly losing myself to this addiction. I was addicted to her violence. I was losing touch with who I was, with what I wanted, with what was important in life. This one time, I was reading this book, *The Five Love Languages* by Gary Chapman, wait, or was it seven languages? A book that was supposed to outline five general ways that romantic partners express and experience love.

This one time, I was reading on the sofa, and she walks in the room, and I tell her enthusiastically, "Look, babe! The Seven Languages of Love!"

Hoping she would also find it exciting and curious to know what love language would define ours, but I had forgotten about her explosive violence.

Maria just walked towards me, angrily snatched the book from my hands, swung the book up to the right with her right arm, and brought it down with the most violent speed against my face. It must have felt like the impact of a brick or a baseball bat across my stupid face. She apologized a few days later, and I forgave her, of course. I needed to break free, or just give in to masochism. Stop on red. Drive on green.

But then, something happened. In one of her violent rages, she told him about our affair. She told me he went crazy and wanted to look for me and kill me. We started seeing each other regularly and stayed the nights. That was the beginning of the end of our relationship. Maybe the thrill of the danger was what kept us together and interested, but it wasn't the same anymore. Maybe she had asked the universe for someone like me to help her break free. Who knows? I guess true love is not just about sex, but about respect, trust, and honesty, something I never really felt with Maria.

Chapter Four: *Gator kisses return, like boomerangs.*

Two years later, I make a right on Biscayne and 33 Street and parked on the side of Biscayne Hotel. In a world full of dogs, where everyone is trying to chase their dreams, I found solace in the Biscayne Hotel. Surrounded by the hustle and bustle of Biscayne Boulevard, it was the perfect place to find inspiration. Picture-perfect days, beautiful women with fashionable smiles, and endless opportunities for adventure were waiting just outside my door. It was the kind of place where a writer could dive into the depths of his imagination and create poetic magic.

And for the first time in a long while, I was happy. Happy to be alive, happy to be in Miami, and most of all, happy to have Carmen in my life. Her curly hair, her cinnamon skin tone, her Spanish accent and the hypnotizing way she danced salsa had influenced my poetry and the way I considered commitment. Sigh. I can honestly say that it felt like the love train had finally arrived at Poetry Love Station after stopping at so many wrong stops with dead-end streets.

The Dodge Dart sat parked on the side of the hotel, and the hotel guests sat at the bar across the pool, laughing and joking around. The four water streams deep-splashing in the pool added to the serene atmosphere of the place.

Today, I could really appreciate the hotel. It felt beachy, antique, and stylish all at once. Relaxing in Miami with style was a luxury I was grateful for. It was nice to know that there was a place for hybrid vagabond poets like us. Mid-century modern architecture inspired the muse in me, and Carmen was always on my mind. It was a hopeful feeling that pushed me off the cliff and propelled me forward with an inspired vagabond spirit.

As I left the hotel towards the Dodge Dart, I saw the Copper-tone girl with her pooch across Biscayne Boulevard. The Biscayne skyline painted against the Miami sky and casting and spilling its beloved shadow on those humid, undulating sidewalks I knew too well.

I took a deep breath and thought to myself, *this is home*.

I got on the Boulevard heading south. The Dodge Dart cruised through the neon lights of motels flickering in the rearview mirror. The Biscayne wind in my lungs was slowly turning me into a wolf ready to howl. Stop on red. Drive on green. I made a left on 25 Street and headed all the way down to the Bay, my daily Miami ritual, to stop and listen to the Bay. I sighed and listened.

I got back on the Dart and headed south on the Boulevard towards 20 Street. Right before making the turn, I realized that I wasn't alone in my car. I could feel the spirit of the Bay sitting next to me, caressing my shoulders as I drove. I was heading over to Kush restaurant to meet Carmen for some gator bites and a beer. Kush was on the corner of North Miami and 20 Street. Driving there, I realized the Biscayne muse didn't only live beneath the waters of Biscayne Bay. She also lived in the Wynwood wind, in the breeze streaming through my Dart, in my sweetheart's loving eyes. Like a blessing and a curse, inside this poet's heart.

Inside Kush, the life-size wall painting of Purvis Young looked through me, so I turned and faced the window instead, looking out at North Miami Ave. We continued sipping on our beers and waited for our gator bites. Glancing out the window, looking at my baby sip on her beer, the beauty of Miami was all around me, and I was finally in tune with it. Immortality could never feel more real. It was a call to action, perhaps, a whisper in the wind, to shake off the lazy wolf syndrome and get back to my Biscayne Hotel to continue writing. But with Carmen by my side, writing would need to wait until I was done giving her all my little gator bite kisses, like the ones I was once a receiver of.

Chapter Five: *Endless Flow. Four Years Later.*

I had just returned from visiting my ailing grandfather in Copan, Honduras. I had decided to stop by my cluttered office at the Vagabond Motel and organize it for a bit. I sat on my writing chair surrounded by piles of papers and empty Styrofoam cups of coffee. Serving myself a cup of coffee and rum, I felt something in my shirt pocket and my memory took me back to when I was saying goodbye to my grandfather at his bedside.

He took my right hand with his cold, shaky, bony hands, placed a small object inside the palm of my hand, closed my hand over the object and said, *"No dejes que nadie te quite esto. Guárdalo, en lugar seguro, que sus poderes mágicos te protegerán a ti y a tu familia."*

I took it out of my shirt pocket, and upon closer inspection, I realized the object was a Mayan artifact of a face with half of it laughing and the other half crying. It was made out of wood and clay, perhaps a symbol representing the passage from one realm to the next. I sighed, drank down the coffee and rum. I placed the artifact inside the drawer of my desk and locked it. The heat and humidity outside were suffocating, but my mind was elsewhere. I thought of my beautiful wife Carmen and our two young daughters, Camila and Victoria. My heart swelled with love for them, and I knew I was the luckiest man in the world to have them by my side.

My thoughts drifted to the day we first met. It was at a poetry reading in a dingy bar in Little Havana, and Carmen's fiery spirit and passion for life had immediately drawn me to her. Even though, in those early days, she was still somewhat emotionally committed to her ex-boyfriend, a low life whose cheating had suddenly ended their relationship. It took me a couple of years to win her heart fully, but once I did, we became inseparable, and I could never imagine my life without her. I loved my wife, but my love for our two daughters was even greater. Their laughter and smiles brought me more joy than any poem ever could. They were my world, my reason for living.

I took a deep breath and felt the words of a new poem starting to form in my mind. I grabbed my typewriter and began to write, letting the words flow freely onto the page.

For me, love was my muse, and my family was my inspiration. If they were by my side, I knew I could conquer anything that life threw my way. I was a poet, and I knew that my words would always flow if love continued to fill my heart—once poisoned but now healed.

While laying on the bed in my Vagabond Motel office, a knock came to the door. Someone knocked three times. I thought, whoever it is, they're going to have to knock six times so I can get up from this cozy bed and answer that door. And while this person knocked the three knocks repeatedly, the more I tried to guess who was behind that door. I had no clue. Finally, the six knocks were about to cue my answering.

I took a deep breath and screamed from my desk, "WHO IS IT?"

Then, I heard a woman's voice.

"Open the fucking door, Oscar!"

I couldn't recognize the voice. I got worried. I got up immediately, put my ear against the door, and I was able to hear another voice whispering. That's when the door exploded and knocked me down to the floor. I hit my head so hard against the wooden floor that my nap must have been about an hour long. When I woke up, I had a pounding pain in the back of my head. I tried to get up from the floor, but someone had nailed my pants and my shirt onto the Florida pinewood floor. I couldn't move at all. My vision was blurry. I couldn't see the faces that surrounded me clearly. Then, I heard the voice of a man.

"Do you want me to chop him up into little pieces, Chacha? Huh? Huh?"

"Beads, calm the fuck down. We just want to scare him, not kill him! Give me the knife and the gun," said Chacha.

"What are you gonna do to him, Chacha? Are you gonna chop him up into little pieces? Huh? Huh?" said Beads.

"Beads! You're annoying the fuck out of me! Get the fuck out of here and go wait for me in the car!"

Somehow, I felt safer without the guy named Beads around. With his exit, the woman closed the door of my office and locked it.

She walked over to me, bent over to face me and said, "I know you're wondering about who we are and why we are doing this to you. It's all very simple, Oscar. We just want you to hand over the Mayan artifact your grandfather gave you. Just give me the artifact and we'll be gone before you know it."

I was so confused. I wondered how they knew I carried the artifact my grandfather had given me. How did they even know about it?

Then, Beads came back into the room.

"Is he talking yet? Did you search the room?"

"Not yet. He's all yours," she said pointing at me, as if giving him permission for something.

She went to the closet and started looking and searching through my clothes and dresser drawers. He was a short bald muscular man with no teeth. His mouth was always open, wrinkled lips hanging, big jaws, and tattoos covering his arms. His face was covered in pimples and small blisters. He had a Russian accent. He stood over me looking deep in my eyes.

I looked at him back and said, "You're a strange looking dude..."

"What did you say, mudderfukker?"

"That you're a strange looking fellow, you fuckhead!" I responded with an anger that came from a disarming fear of dying without fighting for my life.

He threw himself at me and hit my face with his forehead. My nose was bloody and broken.

"I'm a strange looking dude, huh?" he asked while slapping my face hard, but I couldn't feel anything.

My face was numb with a constant shock of pain.

He kept on asking and repeating, "I'm a strange looking dude? I'm a strange looking dude? I'm a strange looking dude? I'm a strange looking dude? Huh? Huh?"

He took hold of the hammer and started removing the nails from the wooden floor. I could feel my shirt and pants loosening from the floor. He kept on repeating the question. I could feel the blood from my nose running down the back of my throat. I was breathing through my mouth. I didn't say anything else to him because I wanted to make sure I was completely loose.

He was fast with the hammer, and while he continued to concentrate on his morbid mantra, I searched the room with my blurry eyes and spotted Chacha sitting on my bed. She had found my Mayan artifact. She held it with her right hand and dialed a number using my cell-phone with her left.

Then, she turned to him and said, "Take him to the bathtub and take off his clothes."

Beads, the mutant, got quiet, grabbed my arms, dragged me all the way to the bathtub, and threw me in there.

I could hear Chacha talking with someone on the phone, but couldn't make out what she was saying. He turned on the hot water and forgot to turn on the cold. I didn't even have the strength to open my eyes. I could feel the hot water burning my skin, and I started waking up slowly from the pain on my face. I wanted to scream, but I couldn't. Chacha came over and started unbuttoning my bloody shirt and pants. I laid there in my boxers, burning under the steamy hot water, feeling more awake. They both just stood there watching me. I noticed she pulled out my artifact from her right pant pocket and gave it to Beads.

"Take this to Tony G, he's waiting for you at Van Orsdel," she said to him.

He turned to go, but she grabbed him from his elbow and pulled him in close.

"If you lose this, Tony will incinerate us both."

He looked at her with his frozen, crazy eyes and said, "I won't fucking lose it. Now let go of my fucking arm."

Beads exited the bathroom, and then the room. Chacha leaned toward me to turn off the hot water. That's when I grabbed her fast from her shoulders and pulled her hard toward me as I rammed my bloody forehead against her face. Then, blackout. The next thing I remember is waking up with her limp body over me. I had knocked us both out. I was able to push her off me with the little strength I had left. I could feel my face pulsating. I crawled out of the bloody tub and pulled my weak body up with the bathroom sink counter.

I looked at myself in the mirror, and my nose looked five times larger with the swelling. I picked up the hammer and the knife from the floor, grabbed my car keys, cell phone, and drove away, peeling my 74 Dodge Dart south on Biscayne towards the crematorium.

I could feel my face pulsating. The adrenaline from my anger was blocking the pain, but it all made perfect sense. Tony G was a hired

Mayan artifact pirate. These had to be the same guys that attacked my grandfather in Honduras. The thought of avenging my grandfather's death made me push the pedal to the metal, and the slant six engine roared past 36 Street and Biscayne at 90mph. I made a sharp right on 34 Street and pulled up on the side of the building with the black smoke chimney.

I got out of the car and realized I was still in my bloody boxers. I went around the back of the crematorium with the hammer in my right hand and the knife in my left. I slowly turned the doorknob, but it was unlocked. I went in slowly, bending my knees and my back, reaching my head quickly up and down to see if I saw something. And there they were. Beads and another guy wearing a metal helmet. To my surprise, I noticed my artifact on a small coffee table next to a couple of car keys right by the back exit door. I quietly grabbed my artifact and the keys. Beads was sitting on a bench, watching that other man with the helmet push a metal stick into a noisy body furnace with a beer in his hand.

I was about to turn away when I noticed a wrinkled, bony hand sticking out from under a white blanket, belonging to a body lying on a stainless-steel bed on wheels. I immediately recognized the hand. It belonged to Vivian, my 83-year-old neighbor, the stripper. Vivian and I were the insomniacs of the rundown apartment building next to the crematorium. We would sit on my windowsill and stare at the black smoke chimney while we sipped on beer, smoked, and imagined the kind of life the person burning had. She was the one that informed me a few months after I moved into that building, that the BBQ smell I was smelling every day was no BBQ. And now the poor thing was laid out on that stretcher.

My anger and sadness made me wish I had a pair of bullets and a gun, but I kept my head low. I needed to crawl all the way to the stretcher and see if it was really Vivian under the blanket.

Suddenly, Beads stood up and said, "I'm gonna go take a shit. These burning bodies are making me feel sick and hungry at the same fucking time."

He walked over to a bathroom door at the opposite end of the furnace area and locked it. The man with the helmet kept pushing and pulling the metal stick into the loud furnace as if in a trance. I stood up slowly and walked over to the body in the blanket, pulled the sheet off the face to see if it was her, and it was her, but to my surprise, she was breathing softly. I could see she had been hit hard on the side of her forehead with something. She wasn't bleeding, but her whole right side of her upper face was purplish red and swollen. I took a deep sigh and squeezed the knife and the hammer with my sweaty hands, turned to look at the man by the furnace, and right when I was about to move, I felt Vivian's cold soft and weak hand grab my left forearm.

I looked at her, and she signaled with her finger on her lips to be quiet. Then, we both heard the toilet flush inside the bathroom. She quickly grabbed the knife from my hand and covered herself with the blanket. I got back on my hands and knees and, like a bloody zombie with fearful eyes, I snuck up behind the man with the metal stick and swung the hammer hard onto the soft back part of his helmet. His body immediately collapsed. That's when Beads opened the bathroom door and saw me standing over the man's body.

"Tony!!! What did you do to Tony? Oh, I'm gonna fucking kill you!!!" Beads screamed, walking towards me fast.

As he passed Vivian, she stood up fast with the knife in hand, and right before Beads reached me, unfolding his arm to punch me, he stopped with his eyes wide open, taking a deep breath. I could see the pointy part of the knife sticking out of the front of his stomach, staining a scarlet red on his shirt and pants. He slowly bent his knees, closing his eyes, and collapsed on top of his buddy, Tony G.

Emotionally defeated and horrified, I put on Tony's helmet, picked up the metal stick, turned off the furnace gas, and in silence, Vivian and I spent the rest of the night feeding the two bodies into the furnace, poking, and breaking the ash. We smoked Tony's cigarettes and drank Beads's beers without saying a word.

That's when I woke up. It was already the next day. I had fallen asleep on my desk, drooling all over a wrinkled pile of my unfinished poems. I had a pounding headache, but I was feeling disoriented and inspired. I picked up the phone and called my wife to let her know I was okay. She asked me where I had been all this time. I told her it was a long story, but that I would be home soon and tell her all about it. I sat in my writing chair and started typing again on the Smith Corona, my grandfather's Mayan artifact tucked safely away in my locked desk.

Poetry & Prose

Truth Is No One Knows The Way You Do

He had been in love with her for as long as he could remember. He didn't know how it happened or when, but he knew that she had stolen his heart and soul with just a smile. And yet, he could never find the courage to tell her how he felt.

So, one day, he wrote her a letter. It was a letter filled with all the things he wanted to say to her, all the feelings that he had been hiding for so long. He sealed the letter and waited for the right moment to give it to her.

Finally, the moment came. They were sitting on a park bench, the sun setting behind them. He took a deep breath and handed her the letter. She looked at him curiously and began to read.
As she read, her face changed from confusion to surprise to joy. She looked up at him, tears in her eyes, and asked him to explain what he meant by the words he had written.

He took her hand in his and spoke from his heart, telling her how much he loved her, how much he admired her, and how much he wanted to spend the rest of his life with her. Emotionally frozen by the fear of rejection.

And then, he asked her the question that had been on his mind for so long: "Will you receive my tongue like a pregnant pope?"

She laughed at the strange question, but he knew that she understood what he meant. He wanted to kiss her, to explore her, to love her in every way possible.

And to his surprise, she said yes. She said that she had been waiting for him to make a move, waiting for him to tell her how he felt. And with those words, they leaned in for a kiss, their tongues exploring each other like two lost souls finding their way home.

It was a kiss that would change their lives forever, a kiss filled with passion, love, and hope. And as they pulled away from each other, they knew that they had found something special, something that would last a lifetime.

"Truth is no one knows the way you do. Ain't that something?" he whispered, looking into her eyes.

"Ain't it?" she replied, smiling back at him.

His Next Move

I remember feeling a wave of paranoia wash over me as I stared at the other me. Was this some sort of hallucination? Had I ingested something strange without realizing it? I rubbed my eyes and pinched myself, but the other me didn't disappear. He just stood there, looking out the window with a serene expression on his face.

I tried to move closer to the mirror, to see if I could touch him or feel some sort of connection between us, but the other me remained out of reach. It was like looking into another dimension, a parallel universe where everything was the same but slightly different. And as I watched, the other me turned his head and looked directly at me.

I felt a shiver run down my spine as our eyes locked. There was something in that gaze that made me feel exposed, like the other me could see right through me. And then, just as suddenly as it had appeared, the other me was gone.

I stumbled back, feeling dizzy and disoriented. Had it all been a trick of the light? A figment of my imagination? I looked back at the mirror, but there was only my own reflection staring back at me. I tried to shake off the feeling of unease that lingered in the pit of my stomach, but I couldn't help feeling like the other me was still out there somewhere, watching me, waiting to make his next move.

Glimmering

I woke up on the floor of my bedroom, sweat pouring down my face, my heart racing like a freight train. What had just happened? Was it a dream or was it real? I stumbled to my feet and went outside, looking up at the sky, hoping for some kind of sign. But there was nothing there except for the moon and the stars, glimmering like they always did.

I went back inside and sat down at my desk, trying to make sense of what had just happened. Was it some kind of hallucination? A fever dream? Or had I really been abducted by aliens?

As I sat there, I realized that I didn't know the answer to any of those questions. All I knew was that something had happened, something that had shaken me to my core. And I knew that I would never be the same again.

I poured myself a glass of bourbon and sat back in my chair, staring off into the distance. The music in my head was still playing, the invisible ray still vibrating inside my chest. And I knew that I would never be able to shake it off.

But maybe that was okay. Maybe that was the price of seeing the world in a different way, of opening yourself up to things that others could never even imagine. Maybe that was what it meant to be truly alive.

As I sat there, sipping on my bourbon, I knew that I was ready for whatever the universe had in store for me. Life or death. Because I had seen things that most people only see in their lucid dreaming, like a highway of information in a higher consciousness realm, multiplied countless of times through our physical selves, like a simulated reality of individual subconsciousness with their own free will.

Sweet Scent Of Freedom

I was trapped in the Armenian jail cell, my billiard ball eyes staring back at me from the metal mirror. The smell of titty-tall greed and the flatulence of despots filled my nostrils, making me gag.

I needed to escape, to find a way out of this hellhole. And then, I noticed it, a faint fruity feminine perfume in the air. I closed one eye, took a deep breath, and aimed. The noise of the jail cell faded away as I focused on the task at hand.

I struck, and the sound of the billiard ball echoed through the cell. But my attention was on the sweet trail of perfume that had caught my nose. I followed it, hoping that it would lead me to freedom.

As I walked, the smell grew stronger, leading me down a dark hallway that I had never noticed before. And then, I saw her, a beautiful woman with flowing brown hair and bright green eyes.

She looked at me with a mixture of fear and sexual curiosity, and I knew that I had to act fast. I grabbed her hand and pulled her along with me, running as fast as we could down the hallway.

We reached a door, and I pushed it open, revealing a staircase that led to the outside. We ran up the stairs, the fresh air filling our lungs as we burst out into the sunlight.

We were free, and I knew that I owed it all to that faint fruity feminine perfume. As we walked away from the jail, I turned to the woman and thanked her for showing me the way.

She smiled at me, her green eyes sparkling in the sun. And as we walked off into the distance, I knew that I had found my way out of the darkness, thanks to her sweet scent leading me to freedom or another sexual, masochistic prison of lust.

The Other Me

Staring in the mirror, I saw someone else appear.
A wave of paranoia left me feeling unclear.
I rubbed my eyes and pinched my arm, but the other me remained.
Like looking in another dimension, everything was the same
but slightly strange.
Our eyes locked, and a shiver down my spine.
Exposed and vulnerable, I felt the divine.
Suddenly, the other me was gone, I was now the one
looking into the other side,
feeling amazed, curious and perplexed.
It was now just me, feeling disoriented and alone.
It was the exact image of my bedroom,
my family photos on the walls,
the same half full glass of water on my nightstand,
and for a split second I couldn't really tell
which one of us was the real me.
Was it real or just my mind?
The unease lingers, hard to unwind.
The other me was still out there,
watching,
waiting,
with a serene stare.

Coy Zebra From Korea

When Jane woke up that morning, she had no idea she would be chasing a zebra from Korea that spurns Japanese corsages. But as she walked to her car, she saw a group of people chasing something down the street. Curious, she went to investigate and saw the zebra, its black and white stripes contrasting against the busy city street.

Jane quickly joined the group, trying to help them catch the elusive animal. It was surprisingly fast and agile, zigzagging between cars and people. But Jane was determined to catch it, spurred on by the adrenaline of the chase.

As they finally caught up to the zebra, it suddenly stopped and turned to face them, its eyes gleaming with a coy intelligence. Jane felt a sudden surge of admiration for the beautiful animal, wondering what it must have gone through to get so far from home.

But before she could contemplate further, the zebra suddenly bolted again, taking off down a nearby alleyway. Jane followed, dodging obstacle past obstacle with the agility of a seasoned athlete.

As they ran, she heard a voice in her head, whispering, "Coy, Trojan horses on the run, leather and nails." She didn't know what it meant, but the words filled her with a strange sense of purpose.

Finally, after what seemed like hours, they cornered the zebra in a dead-end alley. Panting and sweating, Jane looked into its eyes and asked, "Why did you run? Why did you spurn Japanese corsages?"

The zebra simply looked at her and *bah-ed,* as if to say, "Not on my watch."

Jane was confused but she didn't have time to think further as the zebra suddenly charged towards her, its hooves thundering on the pavement. But instead of attacking, it suddenly leapt over her head, leaving behind a small leather pouch that landed at her feet.

As she opened the pouch, she found a note inside that read, "Or, a coy zebra from Korea that spurns Japanese corsages. *Bah!!* Not on my watch. I should have counted slower just to see them fall like leaves. Coy, Trojan horses on the run, leather, and nails. Will you receive my tongue like a pregnant pope? Will you deliver your sin like this always, so early? Truth is no one else knows the way you do. Ain't that something? Ain't it?"

Jane was confused, tranced, and intrigued, wondering what it all meant.

Vivid And Terrifying

I've never been one to believe in the supernatural or unexplained, but that night was different. The sound that woke me up from my slumber was so loud and intense that I knew something was off. Still half-asleep, I stumbled my way to the kitchen, my mind racing with confusion and fear. And then, I saw it. The small, gray figure perched on my kitchen counter, its presence eerie and unsettling. Before I could even react, a beam of light shot out from its eyes, and I was lifted off my feet and pulled towards the craft. Inside, I was held down by two other gray beings, their cold fingers digging into my skin. Painful, inexplicable knowledge was forced into my brain, and I felt helpless as my body was paralyzed. I tried to scream, but nothing came out of my mouth. The next thing I knew, I was surrounded by a kaleidoscope of colors and shapes, trapped inside a gumball machine. At first, I was in awe of the beauty that surrounded me, but soon my joy turned to fear as I realized I couldn't move. My body was stuck, pressed against the glass with a force that made my nose bleed. And then, there was a snap, and everything went black. When I woke up, I was back in my bed, with no memory of how I got there. But the fear and trauma of the abduction stayed with me for the rest of my life, haunting me like a nightmare that I could never fully shake off. It wasn't the first strange occurrence in my life, but it was by far the most vivid and terrifying.

Even After I Am Gone

It was a strange sensation on my arm that started it all. At first, it felt like a hard rock lodged between my skin and muscle, but then it disappeared as quickly as it came. I didn't think much of it until I noticed that my eyes were becoming extremely sensitive to light.

The sensation returned, this time on the left side of my neck, and that's when I knew that something was seriously wrong. I went to see my doctor, who confirmed the presence of a piece of metal inside my skin, but there was no puncture wound to indicate how it got there.

My vision began to deteriorate rapidly, and I went to see my ophthalmologist, but even he couldn't explain the cause of the damage. The most disturbing discovery came from an X-ray of my head, which revealed a mysterious piece of metal on the left side of my frontal lobe.

As the weeks went by, my health deteriorated further. I began to experience blackouts and seizures, and my memory was fading fast. But what scared me most were the vivid dreams that I couldn't shake off. Dreams of a visitation, of a creature that pulled my teeth out one by one, leaving my mouth full of blood.

I knew that my days were numbered. The piece of metal in my brain was slowly killing me, and there was nothing I could do to stop it. But I wanted to leave a record of my experience, a marker for those who would come after me.

And so, I wrote down my story, carving it into my teeth, like rings in a tree. The teeth now sit on my nightstand, a grim testament to the horror that I had experienced. As I take my last breath, I am happy, knowing that my story will be remembered, even after I am gone.

LIGHTS

I remember the day like it was yesterday, though it was years ago. We were driving down I-75, my wife and I, with a storm brewing on the horizon. I had my foot on the pedal, racing against the sunset. We had to make it to Saint Petersburg before nightfall. And then, it happened. The lights descended from the clouds, silent as a thief in the night. They were like nothing I had ever seen before, like a two-story building floating in the sky with bright windows.

Before I knew it, our car had turned off, and we were surrounded by the lights. And then, we woke up on the side of the road, disoriented and confused. My wife was next to me, crying in her sleep. I looked at my watch, and it was already five in the morning. What had happened? Where had we been taken? Were we abducted?

These questions have haunted me ever since that day. I've always felt like they were watching me, following me, studying me. And yet, they never come close enough to touch. I've waited and waited, year after year, hoping that they would take me with them, show me what lies beyond our world. But they never have. Why won't they take me? Am I not special enough?

But I won't wait forever. If they don't come for me, then I'll go to them. I'll find a way to reach them, to show them that I am worthy of their attention. I am not like the two-bit idiots they've taken before. I am different. I am special. And if they won't come to me, then I'll go to them, no matter the cost.

Electric Eels

Once upon a time, there were accountants who wore pajamas to bed, even when they worked. They were so dedicated to their work that they would often stay up all night, pouring over financial statements and crunching numbers. But one day, they stumbled upon a secret that changed everything.

It started with a simple mistake. One of the accountants accidentally spilled milk on his keyboard. As he cleaned it up, he noticed something strange. The milk was disappearing, as if something was drinking it. He looked closer and saw a tiny electric eel, wriggling around in the wires.

Curious, the accountants started experimenting with the eels. They discovered that the eels could generate electricity, which could be harnessed to power their computers. Excited by this discovery, the accountants began stealing milk from the office fridge to feed the eels.

As they continued their experiments, the accountants became increasingly obsessed with the eels. They stopped sleeping and stopped eating, pouring all their time and energy into the project. They even started wearing pajamas to work so they could always be closer to the eels.

But their obsession had consequences. The accountants became pale and gaunt, their eyes dark and sunken. Their colleagues started to worry, but they refused to listen, too focused on their quest to harness the power of the electric eels.

Eventually, the accountants succeeded in their mission. They built a system that could capture and harness the electricity generated by the eels, revolutionizing the way computers were powered. But by then, it was too late for the accountants. They had become so consumed by their obsession that they had lost everything else in their lives.

As the accountants drifted off to sleep, they dreamed of electric eels swimming through a sea of milk. They were taller than their mothers, but they knew that the love they felt for their work was a strange and dangerous thing. They could only hope that someday they would find a way to balance their passion with the rest of their lives and find happiness once again.

Love Is Evil

I am in Miami, lounging in a rattan chair in the humid night air, a cigarette smoldering in my hand. I am thinking about love, as I often do, and how it's the most imperfect thing that possesses me. It's like a devil that sneaks into my heart and sets up camp, corrupting my mind and driving me to do things that others might consider foolish or reckless.

Love is the result of an encounter where dreaming and the lack of physical affection become one for me. It's what stops me in my tracks, what propels me to do what others might consider ridiculously vulnerable. It's a force that makes me create the most beautiful artistic things, and then once I completely convince myself of their beauty, that same love that created it starts destroying it.

But fear is always lurking in the shadows, like a monster waiting to pounce. Sometimes I feel like I'm completely composed of it. Like I am 90% fear and 10% love. Love is the creative light that makes me likable. Fear is the other me that turns into a monster, the one that breaks all the plates, the one that projects his own fear onto others.

Love and sex are like a rock someone throws inside a fishbowl, and the romantic daydreaming fish inside the bowl splashes out of the bowl, not exactly knowing what just happened to him. I am like that fish in the bowl, daydreaming and meditating on the most powerful act of love, just to be thrown out of balance into a perfect drowning of fear.

That's why I'm done with it. I mean, I'll continue writing for others. I'll continue pretending I'm okay with love, even though I never seem to know what it's about. Take, for instance, my long-distance relationship. How can I continue to fall into this impractical pattern of unrequited love and still find an illusion, a made-up fantasy that would fuel a desire for something more appropriate? Practical. Deserving even.

But in the end, love is a lie disguised as a painful truth after all the sweet sex has ended.

In the end, love is evil.

Honey & Sting

The Cock Fight

I remember this one time in Honduras,
when I attended a cock-fighting circus,
the men were eager, waiting for the arrival
of their trained roosters, ready for survival,
respected for their prime fighting cocks.
On the seasoned patio, destiny awaited the cages and the talks,
singing roosters insulted each other with their song
as people made their way onto the patio, walking along.
The humble man who hosted the event
built the ring and chairs with ease and talent,
covered the floor with cedar chips and pine dust,
creating a small ring theater that was robust.
The wife of the host sat behind a wooden counter,
selling oranges, tropical fruits, and beer, with a passive manner.
The cock-fighters drank beer, one after another,
so much so that they laid on the floor, like dead brothers.
The wife, angry with her husband, slammed a beer bottle
to wake everyone up, including the sleeping rooster throttle.
The announcement was made, and the fight began,
two beautiful birds, more elegant than the eagle clan.
The crowd cheered as the birds were thrown in the air,
stabbing each other with their dignified arrows, with flair.
The victor glided down with grace, singing his song of victory,
while the caged cocks sang their annoying cacophony.
Everything was back to normal, the beer was flowing.
As people made a line for more, the time was slowing.
I sat on a homemade stool, waiting for the next match,
enjoying the moment and the memory of the cock-fighting patch.

The Brooklyn Bridge

I arrived in Manhattan with a sense of urgency. The Brooklyn Bridge beckoned to me, promising both adventure and danger. I knew I had to walk across it, to feel the wind and the vibrations of the cars passing beneath me. I had heard the rumors about the middle towers, how they had a power over the mind that could make even the sanest man jump off the bridge. I had to test that theory for myself.

As I made my way to the Brooklyn Bridge, I felt a sense of anticipation building within me. I couldn't wait to feel the rush of adrenaline, to experience the unknown. When I finally reached the entrance, I paused for a moment, taking in the view of the city that lay before me. The skyline was magnificent, and I felt a sense of awe and reverence for this great city.

With a deep breath, I stepped onto the bridge and began to walk across. The sound of the cars passing beneath me was deafening, but I felt invigorated by it. As I reached the middle towers, I felt a strange sensation wash over me. It was as if something bigger than myself had taken hold of my mind, urging me to jump off the bridge.

I don't remember if I jumped that night or if I refused to give in to that urge. I don't know if I continued to walk afterwards—it's all a blur. I do remember my heart pounding with excitement. When I finally reached the other side, I felt a sense of accomplishment wash over me. I had conquered the Brooklyn Bridge, and I felt as though I could conquer anything. Or did that bridge conquer me? And now I will never be able to conquer anything?

That night, I drank heavily with my friends, celebrating our victory over the bridge. We laughed and joked, and I felt a sense of belonging that I had never felt before. As we made our way back through the bridge, I couldn't help but wonder if the stories were true. Did none live to tell the tale of the Brooklyn Bridge?

But I remember feeling determined to be the exception. I had walked across the Brooklyn Bridge, and I had lived to tell the tale, I think.

Or did my friends that night go out drinking with the ghost of me?

In Pleasure

Walking into our hotel room,
I heard Maria in the shower.
The view was stunning, my heart abloom,
and my love for her was devoured.
The room was spacious, a sight to behold,
with a kitchen, dining and living room to explore.
The ocean view was infinite, with waves so bold,
and windsurfers played, leaving me in awe.
The wooden dresser, the table, and the Mezcal
were all we needed to enjoy our stay.
Sliced limes, salt, and shot glasses in the hall,
we indulged ourselves in lovers' play.
Maria emerged from the bathroom,
wrapped in a pink towel, looking divine.
I felt myself consumed by love's perfume,
as I undressed, ready to make her mine.
We enjoyed each other's company, wild and free,
then drifted into a peaceful sleep.
The moon rose slowly, a sight to see,
as we woke up, laughing and carefree.
We had some arguments before,
but here, at this moment, they all disappeared.
No anger or hatred anymore,
only love and pleasure, we cheered.
I left to explore the bars with live music,
and came across the beautiful Sofia and her sound.
Her companion looked at me, a bit too quick,
but I didn't react, no need to be profound.
Back in the room, I saw Maria's legs,
and I felt myself getting excited.
I picked up the bottle, poured myself a shot, feeling delighted.
I shouted, *"I'll eat you, too, just like the worm!"*
and Maria laughed, her joy so pure.
We drank the Mezcal, feeling firm,

in love, in lust, and in pleasure.

Lizard Landlord

It was the summer of 2003,
in an old apartment building,
between Biscayne and Northeast 2nd,
off 33rd. *My home,* I always thought.
With a mentally unstable landlord,
who roamed the halls, gun fully drawn,
and part-time work at a history museum.
My days were busy, never boring.
Shady folks came and went,
prostitutes and pimps, some sent,
and the scent of barbecue lingered.
My neighbor, the stripper, was trigger-fingered.
One day, the phone rang, and I answered.
It was my landlord, my heart was hampered.
He demanded rent, I hung up in disgust.
Asking for money is one thing, cursing another.
A knock came, and my neighbor was there,
a 75-year-old stripper with beer to share.
As we sipped, she spoke of her past,
famous once, now forgotten, her youth didn't last.
We discussed the poetry of life
as the smoke from the chimney was rife.
She pointed, and I saw it too,
outside my window, the chimney grew.
I told her I would check it out,
and she left, without a doubt.
The phone rang again, and it was my landlord,
demanding rent, his voice hard.
He threatened to bomb my door,
but I hung up, not wanting to hear more,
Suddenly, a giant lizard appeared,
wearing sunglasses, shorts, and a funny beard.
It was my landlord, insane and dangerous,
demanding rent, gun loaded and ominous.

We drove to the bank, but it was closed.
His gun was out of his hand, and I froze.
I picked it up, aimed it with a steady hand,
and the lizard ran off in the end.
I drove off into the busy streets,
wondering what the future holds, what it meets.
Back at the apartment, I pondered and mused,
on the shady people and the smoky chimney's ruse.
My summer of 2003 was never dull,
and my landlord, the lizard, was never cool.

A Real Love Story

I remember that book release party like it was yesterday. The wine was flowing freely, the cheese was bountiful, and people were milling about, barely giving the author a second glance. But then, I saw her. Carmen. She was breathtaking. Her eyes were pools of brown sugar, and her smile could light up a room. I was immediately captivated, like a moth to a flame.

We talked, we laughed, and we shared stories. And when the night was over, I walked her to her car, hoping for a chance to see her again. And to my surprise, I did. We ran into each other at Wood Tavern, a place where everyone went to see and be seen. We talked, we drank, and we danced. The chemistry was palpable. We were two magnets, drawn together by an irresistible force.

After that night, we were inseparable. We explored every inch of Miami, from South Beach to Wynwood. We went to concerts, art shows, and movies together. We were two birds in love, soaring over the city, free and unencumbered. And then, one day, we decided to get married. We had a small ceremony at City Hall, just the two of us and a couple of witnesses. It was perfect.

We bought a house in Biscayne Park and started a family. Two beautiful girls, Victoria and Camila. They were our suns, radiating light and joy wherever they went. We watched them grow, our hearts overflowing with love. We were a family, and we were happy.

Now, as we sit on the porch of our house, sipping coffee and watching the girls play, I can't help but think how lucky I am. How lucky we all are. I look at Carmen, and I know. I know that she's my soulmate, my partner, my everything. And as the sun sets over Miami, I lean in and kiss her, and we both know that we'll be together until the end of time.

Cheese

I am a struggling poet, spending most of my days hunched over my typewriter, trying to find the perfect words to express my deepest feelings. One evening, as I was lost in thought, I heard a strange buzzing noise outside my window. I approached the glass and saw a bright light that seemed to be getting closer and closer. Suddenly, a beam of light shot down from the sky and engulfed me. The next thing I knew, I was in a metallic room with no windows or doors, surrounded by tall, gray creatures with big, black eyes. I realized I had been abducted by aliens.

The aliens spoke to me in a language I couldn't understand, and they examined me with strange devices. Despite my fear, I felt a strange sense of calm washing over me. I knew there was nothing I could do to escape, so I surrendered to the experience and allowed myself to be taken. Hours, maybe days, pass, and I lost track of time. When I finally found myself back in my tiny apartment, I was disoriented and confused. But I also felt something new and powerful stirring inside me. I felt a deep love for the world and everyone in it, a love that I knew had been planted in me by aliens.

I sit down at my typewriter and begin to write. Words flow from me like never before, and I find myself writing the cheesiest, most romantic poetry I have ever produced. I write about a love that can conquer the stars, about lovers lost and found, about the beauty of the world and the people in it. As I write, I know that something fundamental has changed inside me. I have been abducted by aliens, but in the process, I have been given a gift—a gift of love that I will carry with me for the rest of my life, the way I carry this cheese.

In The Universe Of Her Love

A thousand flowers blooming, new, tender, pink, and moist.
Love, a crystal dissolving, in the universe of her voice.
Nonsense and intelligence, both valued with care.
The sweet pain of blooming, with lips that both sting and share.
Invisible metronomes ticking, twenty minutes, but what are they?
Memories of love, music, and writing, her kisses left to guide my way.
Prints of her bare feet on my floor, the trail of her perfume in my room.
Disappearing wings on my back, slowly bringing me back to the womb.
Questions stick like fishhooks, longing for her touch and sight.
But I hold on to the one hundred kisses,
left on my body as proof of her might.
She is the bee and the honey, the moon blue and fragrant above.
And I am the crystal dissolving,
in the universe of her love.

Stardust

The bourbon arrived and I slid it over to her.
She took a sip and licked her lips slowly.
I could feel my own lips parting in response,
and I quickly took a gulp of my beer.
I continued to write about her,
my words flowing like a river as I delved deeper
into her enigmatic nature.
She seemed to be listening intently,
her eyes never leaving mine.
Suddenly, she leaned forward and whispered in my ear,
"Do you want to see something truly out of this world?"
I felt a shiver run down my spine as I nodded,
and she stood up and beckoned me to follow her.
We walked out into the raging storm,
the rain drenching us to the bone.
But I didn't care.
I was entranced by this meteorite girl, this Carmen,
and I would follow her anywhere.
She led me to the edge of the beach,
where the waves were crashing against the shore.
"Watch," she said, and then she lifted her arms up to the sky.
In that moment, the storm parted,
and a beam of light descended from the clouds and enveloped her.
I watched in awe as her body began to glow even brighter,
her form blurring and shifting until she was no longer human at all.
Instead, she had transformed into a being of pure energy,
radiating light and power.
I fell to my knees in front of her,
overwhelmed by the sheer magnitude of what I was witnessing.
She seemed to understand and reached out a hand to touch my face.
I felt a surge of electricity course through my body,
and I knew that I would never be the same again.
When I woke up the next morning, I was lying on the beach,
the storm had long gone.

But the memory of Carmen, the meteorite girl,
burned in my mind, immediately and forever.
I knew that I would spend the rest of my life searching for her,
chasing after that sense of wonder and magic that she had brought into
my life.
Lightning.
Thunder.
And the memory of a girl
who had fallen to Earth
and changed everything.

Sand Between My Teeth

I wake up on the beach,
the taste of sand between my teeth.
It plays like an extended long play record made of fish skin,
crunchy like the bark of pigs at Sunday service.
I try to spit it out, but it's too ingrained in my mouth.
As I get up and walk along the shore,
the sand continues to pulse in my mouth,
creating an old sound with each chew.
The smell of charred skin fills my nostrils,
reminiscent of bacon cooking at 2 A.M.
I wonder how long I have been asleep on the beach,
and what has caused me to wake up with sand in my mouth.
As I walk further down the beach,
I see a group of people gathered around a bonfire.
The smell of bacon grows stronger,
and I realize that they are cooking breakfast.
I approach them, hoping to find some answers.
They welcome me with open arms,
offering me a plate of bacon and eggs.
As I eat, I ask them how long I have been asleep on the beach,
and they tell me that it has been a whole day and night.
I am shocked, wondering how I could have slept for so long.
They tell me that they found me on the beach
and that I had been unconscious with the sand between my teeth.
As I finish my breakfast, I realize
that I have been given a second chance at life.
The sand between my teeth, the bacon cooking over the bonfire,
and the sound of the waves crashing against the shore
are all reminders of the beauty and fragility of life.
I thank the strangers for their kindness
and promise to never take another moment for granted.
And as I walk away from the beach,
with the taste of sand still lingering in my teeth,
I know that I have been given

a new perspective on life,
but what the fuck.

Monday Runs Wild

Monday runs wild, and I'm trapped in this hotel. The guests are like vultures, circling the pool, fighting for scraps of sun. I wish I were a hundred poems deep, with the words to capture the beauty of this place, but all I have is this ache in my chest.

I check out of my room at 11 a.m,, but the odds of beating this place are thin. Ten blocks away, my apartment by the bay waits for me, calling to me with the salty breeze.

But I'll miss this place. I'll miss the comfort of this Cadillac bed, the way it made me feel like a hybrid vagabond, ready to settle down and stay forever. But I can hear the boulevard calling to me, the sound of passing cars like the howling of a pack of wolves. It stirs something in me, something wild and restless.

I'm ready to move on, but I don't want to. Do I have to?

I pack my bags slowly, savoring the last moments in this room. I remember the moments I spent here, the memories that I've made. The laughter, the tears, the late-night conversations that spilled into the early hours of the morning.

But it's time to go. I sling my bags over my shoulder and head out into the hallway. The walls are closing in on me, the fluorescent lights flickering overhead. I can't wait to be out of here.

As I step outside, the heat hits me like a punch in the gut. The air is thick with humidity, and the sun beats down on me. I shield my eyes and look up at the sky, searching for some kind of solace.

But then, I hear it again, the howling of the cars on the boulevard.
It's a sound that fills me with a sense of urgency,
a need to keep moving forward.

Scenes Like These

This is our last image,
a farewell at the Poetry Station.
The crowded people oppress,
weighing on our small masterpiece.
I'll tell you everything tonight,
as I reach the ungrateful age.
You're not the same girl I met,
and even our love has changed.
The insurrection's sad face
smiles at me for yours.
Our love cannot sprout
on this hot, hurricane-stirred land.
The remains pile up,
waiting for my adjectives.
I prefer exact observation,
over sentimental declarations.
The Poetry Station is an open book,
with scenes like these to spare.

Out There

I wake up on the floor of my bedroom,
sweat pouring down my face,
my heart racing like a freight train.
What just happened?
Is it a dream or is it real?
I stumble to my feet and go outside,
looking up at the sky, hoping for some kind of sign.
But there is nothing there
except for the moon and the stars,
glimmering like they always do.
I go back inside and sit down at my desk,
trying to make sense of what just happened.
Is it some kind of hallucination?
A fever dream?
Or have I really been abducted by aliens?
As I sit here, I realize
that I don't know the answer to any of those questions.
All I know is that something happened,
something that shook me to my core.
And I know that I will never be the same again.
I pour myself a glass of bourbon
and sit back in my chair,
staring off into the distance.
The music in my head
is still playing,
the invisible ray
still vibrating inside my chest.
And I know that I will never be able to shake it off.
But maybe that's okay.
Maybe that's the price
of seeing the world in a different way,
of opening myself up to things
that others could never even imagine.
Maybe that's what it means

to be truly alive.

Other Works by Oscar Fuentes

Beautiful Women Will Never Know (2013)
4 Nights With Betsy (2014)
Vagabond: Selected Poems, Short Stories, and Plays (2015)
Welcome Home: Poems inspired by 1Hotel South Beach (2019)
For the Love of Leotards (2022)

Other Works Featuring Oscar Fuentes

Body Furnace (2021)
The Cock Fight (2022)
Oscar The Clown (2022)

About the Author

Born in Manhattan, New York, to immigrant parents from Honduras, Oscar Fuentes is a multidisciplinary artist based in Miami, who has been sharing his talents and love of the arts for more than 30 years. Known by his moniker, The Biscayne Poet, Oscar has dedicated more than three decades to sharing his talents and passion for the arts. He is the author of eight books of poetry and prose, including *Beautiful Women Will Never Know* (2013), *4 Nights With Betsy* (2014), *Vagabond: Selected Poems, Short Stories, and Plays* (2015), *Welcome Home: Poems inspired by 1Hotel South Beach* (2019), and *For the Love of Leotards* (2022). Oscar has also been featured in illustrated zine publications such as, *Body Furnace* (2021), *The Cock Fight* (2022), and *Oscar The Clown* (2022).

Oscar was most recently honored by Mayor Daniella Levine Cava with the inaugural Miami-Dade Mayoral Poetry Commendation in recognition of outstanding contributions to the county's literary art community. He is represented by Eaton Literary Agency and uses typewriter tape for a mustache.

Connect with Oscar on Social: @thebiscaynepoet

www.thebiscaynepoet.com

About the Publisher

Indie Earth Publishing is an independent, author-first
co-publishing company based in Miami, FL, dedicated to giving au-
thors and writers the creative freedom they
deserve. Indie Earth combines the freedom of
self-publishing with the support and backing of traditional publishing
for poetry, fiction, and short story collections by providing a plethora
of services meant to aid them in the book publishing experience. With
Indie Earth Publishing, you are more than just another author, you are
part of the Indie Earth creative family,
making a difference one book at a time.

www.indieearthbooks.com

Instagram: @indieearthbooks

For inquiries, please email:
indieearthbooks@gmail.com

About the Type

This book was set in Garamond, a typeface created by and named for Claude Garamond, a sixteenth-century Parisian engraver and typefounder. A perennial masterpiece of old type serif, Garamond is distinguished by its graceful irregularity among individual letters and contrast between light and heavy strokes, which gives the sense of a calligrapher's handwriting. This version of Garamond, EB Garamond, was designed by Robert Slimbach, who captured the gracefulness of the original Garamond typefaces while creating a typeface family that is well suited for comtemporary digital printing.